CYBERSECURITY
PLAYBOOK
FOR EXECUTIVES

CYBERSECURITY PLAYBOOK
FOR EXECUTIVES

ANIS TRABELSI

PALMETTO
PUBLISHING
Charleston, SC
www.PalmettoPublishing.com

Hardcover ISBN: 979-8-8229-5442-7
Paperback ISBN: 979-8-8229-5443-4
eBook ISBN: 979-8-8229-5444-1

CONTENTS

Introduction · vii

Section 1: The Role of Leadership in Cybersecurity · · · · · · · · · · · · · · 1
Chapter 1   The Role of CIO· 2
Chapter 2   The CIO and CEO's Relationship · · · · · · · · · · · · · · · 7
Chapter 3   The CIO and CISO's Relationship · · · · · · · · · · · · · 9
Chapter 4   C-Suite and Executive Buy-In · · · · · · · · · · · · · · 11

Section 2: Building a Strong Cybersecurity Foundation· · · · · · · · · · 13
Chapter 5   GRC in Hospitals· 14
Chapter 6   HIPAA and Health-Care Compliance · · · · · · · · · · · 17
Chapter 7   NIST and CIS Frameworks· · · · · · · · · · · · · · · · · · 23
Chapter 8   Incident Response Plan and Disaster Recovery
              Procedures · 27
Chapter 9   Medical Devices and Cyber Threats · · · · · · · · · · · 31
Chapter 10 Artificial Intelligence (AI) in Health Care · · · · · · · · · 36
Chapter 11 Mastering the Cybersecurity Life Cycle · · · · · · · · · · 42

Section 3: Collaborative Approaches to Cybersecurity · · · · · · · · · · 45
Chapter 12 Building a Team · 46
Chapter 13 Consultant Partnerships · · · · · · · · · · · · · · · · · 49
Chapter 14 Relationships with Law Enforcement and Other
              Government Agencies· · · · · · · · · · · · · · · · · · · 52
Chapter 15 Cyber Insurance · 55
Chapter 16 Vendor Assessments · · · · · · · · · · · · · · · · · · · 57

Conclusion · 60
Acknowledgments· 62

INTRODUCTION

When my boss offered me the role of chief information officer, I was equally honored and apprehensive. I had spent a few years honing my skills in cybersecurity as the chief security officer, but the truth was, I lacked the traditional experience one might expect of someone assuming such a pivotal leadership position. However, my boss saw something in me that went beyond a mere checklist of qualifications. She recognized my unwavering dedication, my keen ability to learn and adapt, and my passion for protecting the digital realm. In offering me this opportunity, my boss demonstrated an extraordinary level of trust—a trust that I vowed to validate through my tireless efforts and commitment to excellence. Her faith in my potential was both humbling and invigorating, driving me to push beyond my perceived limitations and embrace the challenges that lay ahead. It was a vote of confidence that I would not take lightly and one that would shape my approach to leadership, emphasizing collaboration, building amazing teams, continual learning, and a steadfast determination to exceed expectations at every turn.

As I sit down to compose this book's introduction, I find myself thinking back on my journey into the intriguing and dynamic world of cybersecurity and information technology in health care.

Technology's potential to bring people and ideas together globally has always interested me. But as our dependence on digital systems increases, so does the threat from bad actors looking to take advantage of weaknesses for their own gain. My enthusiasm for cybersecurity, which is the first line of defense against those attempting to infiltrate our digital infrastructure, steal our data, and upend our way of life, was sparked by this insight.

In the last few years, I have had the honor of working with some of the most brilliant brains in IT and cybersecurity (my IT department, my cyber team, or "my cyber ninjas," as I call them; and some of the best third-party vendors in the industry) who are always coming up with new ways to stay one step ahead of the competition and adjusting to new threats.

The information and experience contained in this book have been combined to create a thorough playbook or guide that will assist C-suite executives, senior leaders, and organizations in navigating the complicated cybersecurity landscape and safeguarding their most important assets.

Regardless of your field, your experience level, or where you are in your career, I hope this book will provide you with the knowledge and skills you need to tackle the obstacles ahead with courage and fortitude.

SECTION 1:
THE ROLE OF
LEADERSHIP IN
CYBERSECURITY

CHAPTER 1:
THE ROLE OF CIO

As the chief information officer (CIO) of a large hospital system, I believe it is crucial to strike a balance between technology, cybersecurity, and business needs. The digital age has ushered in a new era of challenges for organizations, where the CIO and their team serve as vigilant navigators steering through the unpredictable waters of the cyber threat landscape. Holding the position of CIO in health care is a unique opportunity to understand how the system works and delivers care and appreciate the importance of the IT department in achieving value and improving the delivery of patient care, which will ultimately lead to better patient outcomes.

CIOs are influential executives who, with the help of their teams, will drive the future of health-care systems and will influence and shape how health care is delivered. CIOs have preponderant visions that go beyond everyday technology challenges and problem-solving. As a CIO, I know my job is to lead my teams, inspire them, influence them, and motivate them to do a very demanding job.

Let's delve into the multifaceted responsibilities of the CIO, exploring the evolving nature of cyber threats, health-care-specific vulnerabilities, and the pivotal role of the CIO in leading cybersecurity initiatives. From traditional hacking methods to sophisticated ransomware attacks, we must remain abreast of the latest tactics employed by cyber adversaries.

An Overview of the Evolving Nature of Cyber Threats

In recent years, the growing threat of cyberattacks has become a pervasive concern for industries across the globe. With the increasing reliance on digital technologies and interconnected systems, businesses are exposed to a myriad of potential vulnerabilities that malicious actors exploit for financial gain, industrial espionage, or even political motives. The sophistication of cyberattacks has risen significantly, with threat actors employing advanced techniques such as ransomware, phishing, and zero-day exploits to compromise organizational networks. This evolving landscape poses a risk to sensitive data, intellectual property, and operational continuity, making cybersecurity a top priority for industries ranging from finance and health care to manufacturing and energy.

The proliferation of interconnected devices and the rise of integrated systems have further amplified the threat landscape. As industries embrace digital transformation and adopt smart technologies, the attack surface expands, providing cybercriminals with more entry points to exploit. The potential consequences of successful cyberattacks on our essential services can be severe, leading to widespread disruptions, economic losses, and even threats to public safety.

Despite efforts to enhance cybersecurity measures, the cat-and-mouse game between defenders and attackers continues to escalate. State-sponsored cyber warfare, organized cybercrime syndicates, and hacktivist groups are among the diverse range of actors contributing to the growing complexity of cyber threats. As industries grapple with the ever-evolving nature of these attacks, collaboration between governments, businesses, and cybersecurity experts becomes crucial to developing effective strategies and sharing threat intelligence. The continual evolution of the cyber threat landscape demands a proactive and adaptive approach to cybersecurity to safeguard the interests of businesses, governments, and the general public alike.

Cybersecurity in the Health-Care Sector

Moving deeper into the exploration, we zone in on the health-care sector, where the stakes are exceptionally high because of the sensitivity of patient data. In the rapidly advancing digital landscape, the health-care industry finds itself at the forefront of an ongoing battle against an ever-evolving spectrum of cyber threats. Historically, health-care organizations have been known for their focus on technology and innovation. However, the proliferation of electronic health records, the interconnectivity of medical devices, and the rise of telehealth have made health-care systems more vulnerable to cyberattacks. According to a recent study, 89 percent of health-care organizations reported around forty-three cyberattacks per year, almost one attack a week.[1] Cybercriminals will continue to target health-care systems more frequently, and the resulting breaches have significant consequences, including loss of sensitive patient data, reputational damage, and operational disruptions.

As we dive into the specifics of cyber threats in the health-care sector, the following are unique challenges and vulnerabilities faced by our organization. Recognizing the intricacies of health-care-specific threats is integral to formulating targeted strategies to fortify our defenses and ensure the security of patient data and critical health-care services. "Ransomware and hacking are the primary cyber threats in health care. Over the past five years, there has been a 256 percent increase in large breaches reported to OCR involving hacking and a 264 percent increase in ransomware."[2]

- **Ransomware's Impact on Patient Care**

    In health care, the impact of ransomware extends beyond financial losses to directly affect patient care. Disruption of

1 https://www.healthcareitnews.com/news/direct-line-between-hospital-cyberattacks-and-patient-mortality-report-shows.
2 https://www.hhs.gov/about/news/2024/03/13/hhs-office-civil-rights-issues-letter-opens-investigation-change-healthcare-cyberattack.html.

critical services, loss of access to patient records, and potential delays in lifesaving procedures highlight the severity of ransomware threats in our industry. Our defense strategies must encompass not only data recovery but also maintaining seamless patient care during and after such incidents.

- **Multiple Systems Challenges**

  The proliferation of interconnected medical devices and systems introduces unique security challenges. Insecurely configured or outdated devices can serve as gateways for unauthorized access, posing risks to patient safety and data integrity. Collaborating with device manufacturers, implementing stringent access controls, and conducting regular security assessments are key to mitigating these specific vulnerabilities.

- **The Human Factor**

  The sensitive nature of health-care data makes insider threats a critical concern. Whether inadvertent or malicious, actions by employees can compromise patient data confidentiality and integrity. Ongoing education, strict access controls, and robust monitoring mechanisms are essential components of our strategy to mitigate insider threats and uphold the trust placed in our health-care system.

- **Regulatory Compliance and Cybersecurity**

  The health-care sector operates under stringent regulatory frameworks designed to protect patient information. Noncompliance not only invites legal repercussions but also exposes our organization to heightened cyber risks. Aligning our cybersecurity practices with regulatory requirements not only ensures legal adherence but also strengthens our overall defense against evolving threats.

- **Emerging Technologies and Security Adaptation**

  Embracing emerging technologies, such as artificial intelligence and machine learning in diagnostics and treatment, introduces additional considerations for cybersecurity. As we integrate these technologies into our health-care ecosystem, it is imperative to concurrently assess and address the evolving threats and vulnerabilities associated with their implementation.

  Understanding the health-care-specific nuances of cyber threats allows us to tailor our cybersecurity strategy to effectively safeguard patient data and uphold the integrity of critical health-care services. By remaining vigilant, adaptive, and collaborative, we can successfully navigate the intricate landscape of cyber threats in the health-care industry.

  Addressing the dynamic nature of cyber threats requires collaboration within our organization and across the health-care industry. Sharing threat intelligence, best practices, and lessons learned enhances our collective cybersecurity resilience. As the CIO, I remain committed to fostering a culture of collaboration and information sharing to stay ahead of emerging threats.

CHAPTER 2:

THE CIO AND CEO'S RELATIONSHIP

In the realm of modern health care, where the digitization of patient records and the integration of cutting-edge technologies are paramount, the relationship between the CIO and the chief executive officer (CEO) is a linchpin for the success of our organization.

In the ever-evolving landscape of cybersecurity threats, our collaboration isn't just a formality; it's a strategic imperative. The CEO and I understand that the health-care industry is a prime target for cyberattacks. Our conversations extend beyond mere budgetary approvals for cybersecurity measures; they delve into a shared vision of ensuring the resilience and integrity of our digital infrastructure. In regular strategy sessions, we assess the evolving threat landscape and align our goals to fortify our defenses against potential breaches.

Moreover, the CEO recognizes that the role of the CIO is no longer confined to the server room. It's about innovating for better patient care, optimizing operational efficiency, and staying ahead of the technological curve. Our partnership isn't just about safeguarding data; it's about leveraging technology to enhance the overall health-care experience. We discuss the implementation of new technologies and ensure that these innovations align with our organizational objectives.

The symbiotic relationship between the CIO and CEO is also reflected in our approach to budgeting. The CEO understands that investing in robust IT infrastructure and cybersecurity measures isn't just an expense; it's also an investment in the long-term sustainability and reputation of the hospital system. We collaboratively prioritize IT needs, balancing immediate concerns with strategic, forward-looking initiatives.

Part of your role as an IT/cyber executive is to make sure your CEO understands where your organization stands as far as cybersecurity measures; the CEO has varying concerns, and you have to ensure they understand the priorities of your department. Only then will they be able to champion budget approvals on your behalf.

In board meetings and steering committees, the CEO and I present a united front, emphasizing the significance of cybersecurity and the broader technology landscape. This not only reassures stakeholders but also fosters a culture of awareness and accountability throughout the organization. Our commitment to transparency in communicating cyber threats and mitigation strategies resonates with both staff and patients, building trust and confidence.

In essence, the CIO-CEO partnership in our hospital system is not merely about ticking boxes in compliance checklists; it's about proactively steering the organization through the complex and dynamic world of health-care IT. Together, we create an environment where innovation is embraced, cybersecurity is a priority, and the overall digital health ecosystem thrives, ensuring that our patients receive the best care possible in a secure and technologically advanced environment.

CHAPTER 3:

THE CIO AND CISO'S RELATIONSHIP

Every corporation creates its hierarchy of executive positions differently, but in health care, with the importance of the balance between technology and cybersecurity, the real question is this: Where should the chief information security officer (CISO) sit within the chain of command? Should they report to the CIO, legal, or compliance?

Of the health-care CISOs I personally know, half of them report to the CIO; the other half report to someone in the compliance or legal department. In my humble opinion and in the health-care IT gold standard, the CISO should report to the CIO. Some experts would argue that the priorities of CIOs and CISOs are different; however, I believe that though the roles might be different, they are definitely intertwined. They are two sides of the same coin.

If there is a good relationship/collaboration/agreement between the CIO and the CISO, then the organization has a better chance of being protected, aligned, and successful. When the CISO reports to the CIO and has a close relationship, then not only is it easier to get budget items approved, but the CISO is also now viewed as a peer in the IT department and not just an enforcer of the rules and policies (better known as "the office of no").

The CIO is responsible for the strategy of the organization and works hand in hand with the CEO to align the right type of technology with the overall road map and goals of the organization. In the last several years, there has been an escalation of security-related issues in the health-care industry. All security responsibilities need to be handled by a CISO, who should report to the CIO. All day-to-day operations of the entire health-care system need to be under a chief technology officer (CTO), and all the planning of clinical strategy and clinical optimization needs to be under the management of a chief medical information officer (CMIO). A successful CIO in a health-care system needs to have these three components reporting to them and leaving the strategic oversight to the CIO.

CHAPTER 4:

C-SUITE AND EXECUTIVE BUY-IN

As health-care IT executives, we recognize the importance of cybersecurity, but other leaders do not always understand the challenges of security. Too often, business executives focus solely on business needs without fully understanding the risks and threats that come with implementing new technologies. This can result in a situation where security is an afterthought, and the organization is left vulnerable to attack.

To fortify an organization's cybersecurity posture, the CIO must secure buy-in from the C-suite and board of directors. I have made a concerted effort to engage other executives in conversations about cybersecurity, to provide training and education, and to involve them in our cybersecurity strategy development.

I am a part of one of the few hospitals that has created in-depth cybersecurity playbooks not just for the IT department but also for each business owner. I have found that engaging other executives in this way has been crucial in shifting our organization's culture toward prioritizing cybersecurity. It is not uncommon for IT departments to be left out of the loop when it comes to business technology contracts until it is too late. I have championed IT involvement in the contract negotiation process from the beginning. Our IT department must review the functionality of the new technology and assess its compatibility with existing systems. It can also identify potential security risks and work with the vendor to address them before the technology is implemented. This vetting process also allows for timelier incident response.

By involving other executives in our cybersecurity strategy development, we have helped them gain a deeper understanding of the risks and threats facing our organization and become more invested in our security programs. They are now more likely to support and advocate for cybersecurity initiatives and to ensure that their teams are following our security policies and procedures. I encourage other health-care organizations to follow our example and prioritize cybersecurity in their own organizations.

SECTION 2: BUILDING A STRONG CYBERSECURITY FOUNDATION

CHAPTER 5:

GRC IN HOSPITALS

In the complex and highly regulated world of health care, where patient well-being is paramount, hospitals must navigate a multitude of challenges, ranging from medical advancements to data security and regulatory compliance. Governing these multifaceted aspects requires a systematic approach, and that's where governance, risk management, and compliance (GRC) frameworks emerge as indispensable tools.

Governance involves establishing and maintaining policies and procedures to guide the institution, risk management focuses on identifying and mitigating potential threats, and compliance ensures adherence to legal and regulatory requirements.

Governance

In hospitals, effective governance sets the tone for organizational culture and decision-making. This includes defining roles and responsibilities, establishing policies for patient care, and ensuring alignment with the institution's mission. For a CEO and the board, governance provides the structure needed to oversee and guide the hospital's strategic direction.

Risk Management

Hospitals face a myriad of risks, ranging from clinical and operational to financial and reputational. Risk management within GRC involves identifying, assessing, and prioritizing these risks. For example, clinical risks may involve patient safety protocols, while financial risks could include budgetary constraints. The risk department plays a pivotal role in developing strategies to mitigate these risks, safeguarding both the hospital's reputation and patient outcomes.

Compliance

Compliance within GRC ensures that hospitals adhere to an ever-evolving landscape of laws, regulations, and industry standards. One of the most critical compliance frameworks in health care is the Health Insurance Portability and Accountability Act (HIPAA), designed to protect patient privacy and data security. Compliance officers work diligently to interpret and implement these regulations, ensuring that hospitals meet legal requirements and avoid penalties.

The Crucial Role of Controls

Controls are the linchpin within the GRC framework. They are the mechanisms put in place to manage risks, enforce policies, and ensure compliance. In hospitals, controls manifest in various forms:

1. *Information Security Controls*

With the increasing digitization of health-care records, robust information security controls are imperative. These controls include encryption, access controls, and regular security audits to protect patient data from unauthorized access and cyber threats.

2. *Clinical Protocols and Quality Controls*

Controlling the quality of patient care involves implementing clinical protocols and standards. From medication administration to surgical procedures, hospitals establish controls to ensure adherence to evidence-based practices, minimizing medical errors and optimizing patient outcomes.

3. *Financial Controls*

Financial controls are crucial for maintaining fiscal responsibility. These include budgetary controls, audit processes, and financial reporting mechanisms to ensure transparency and accountability in the allocation of resources.

4. *Compliance Audits and Monitoring*

Regular compliance audits and monitoring mechanisms are essential components of GRC. These controls ensure that hospitals continually meet regulatory requirements, allowing for early detection and correction of potential compliance gaps—mainly those outlined by HIPAA, which will be covered in the next chapter.

CHAPTER 6:
HIPAA AND HEALTH-CARE COMPLIANCE

The Health Insurance Portability and Accountability Act (HIPAA) plays a crucial role in health-care compliance. HIPAA establishes national standards for protecting the privacy and security of individuals' medical records and other personal health information (PHI). Health-care organizations, including hospitals, clinics, insurance companies, and other covered entities, are required to comply with HIPAA regulations to safeguard the confidentiality and integrity of patient data. Failure to comply with HIPAA can result in significant financial penalties, legal consequences, and damage to an organization's reputation. Consequently, health-care compliance professionals must ensure that their organizations have implemented appropriate administrative, technical, and physical safeguards to meet HIPAA requirements and protect sensitive patient information from unauthorized access, use, or disclosure.

Understanding HIPAA's Significance
HIPAA, enacted in 1996, has become a cornerstone for safeguarding patient data privacy and security in the United States. As we are the custodians of a massive repository of sensitive patient information, the onus falls heavily on our shoulders to ensure compliance with HIPAA regulations. This involves not only the protection of electronic health records but also the implementation of comprehensive safe-

guards to secure patient confidentiality across all facets of our digital infrastructure.

From an operational standpoint, HIPAA compliance significantly influences our decision-making at every turn. The implementation of new technologies, the adoption of innovative software solutions, and even the structuring of internal workflows all must align seamlessly with the strictures of HIPAA. A breach of compliance not only exposes our institution to severe legal consequences but also, more importantly, jeopardizes the trust that patients place in our ability to safeguard their sensitive health information.

Patient Trust and Confidentiality

At the heart of the health-care profession is the sacred trust between patients and their health-care providers. HIPAA reinforces this trust by establishing stringent guidelines for the handling, storage, and transmission of patient data. Patients must feel secure in the knowledge that their medical records are confidential and protected from unauthorized access.

As the health-care industry becomes increasingly globalized, adherence to HIPAA standards also positions our institution as a responsible global player in data protection. Patients from different parts of the world seeking health-care services can rest assured that their data is handled with diligence and care, aligning with internationally recognized principles of data protection. This includes encryption of sensitive patient data, both in transit and at rest; securing data as it moves between different systems; and ensuring that stored data is encrypted to prevent unauthorized access in case of a breach.

Beyond legal and regulatory obligations, HIPAA embodies ethical considerations in the digital age. Respecting patient autonomy and empowering individuals to have control over their health information is central to the ethos of HIPAA. This emphasis on ethical data practices not only complies with the law but also aligns with the ethical principles inherent in the practice of medicine.

The Integration of Compliance into IT Strategy

As a CIO, I know weaving compliance considerations into the fabric of our IT strategy is imperative. This means that from the inception of any technological initiative, compliance is not an afterthought but an integral part of the planning process. Whether it be the deployment of cloud-based systems and integration devices or the development of telehealth platforms, each step is taken with meticulous attention to maintaining HIPAA compliance.

In an era of interconnected health-care systems, the ability to share patient information seamlessly is crucial for delivering comprehensive and timely care. HIPAA provides a standardized framework for data exchange and facilitates interoperability while ensuring that patient privacy remains paramount. This interconnectedness enhances the quality of care and promotes better health outcomes.

Striking a delicate balance between fostering technological innovation and maintaining patient privacy is a constant challenge. HIPAA serves as a guidepost, delineating the boundaries within which technological advancements must operate. This ensures that while we harness the power of cutting-edge technologies, we do so responsibly, without compromising the sanctity of patient information.

Investment in Security Infrastructure

A robust and resilient security infrastructure becomes integral in the quest for compliance. Investment in state-of-the-art cybersecurity measures, regular audits, and continual staff training are essential components of our strategy to fortify our defenses against potential threats. The interplay between technological advancements and compliance requirements demands a proactive approach, where security measures are not just reactionary but anticipate potential risks.

Ensuring compliance is not a one-time event but an ongoing commitment. Regular collaboration with legal experts, compliance officers, and regulatory bodies is vital to staying abreast of evolving requirements. The health-care industry is dynamic, with regulations subject to change. Hence, our decision-making processes must be agile, capable of adapting to shifting compliance landscapes.

Legal and Reputational Ramifications

Noncompliance with HIPAA can result in severe legal consequences, including hefty fines and penalties. However, the impact goes beyond financial implications. A breach can tarnish the reputation of the health-care institution, eroding the trust of both current and potential patients. The repercussions can be long-lasting, affecting not only the bottom line but also the overall standing of the hospital in the community.

A Few Ways to Manage HIPAA Compliance

Effective HIPAA compliance management requires a multifaceted approach that involves ongoing efforts from health-care organizations. It starts with conducting a comprehensive risk assessment to identify potential vulnerabilities and areas of noncompliance within the organization's processes, systems, and workforce. Based on the findings, organizations must develop and implement robust policies, procedures, and safeguards to address the identified risks and ensure the privacy and security of protected health information (PHI). Regular training and awareness programs for employees are essential to foster a culture of compliance and maintain vigilance against evolving cyber threats. Additionally, organizations should establish mechanisms for continuous monitoring, auditing, and timely remediation of any compliance issues that may arise. By adopting a proactive and systematic approach, health-care entities can effectively navigate the complex landscape of HIPAA regulations and maintain the trust of their patients.

A. Regular Risk Assessments and Audits

Periodic risk assessments and audits are essential to identify vulnerabilities and gaps in security. Regularly auditing systems and processes ensures ongoing compliance with HIPAA standards. The CIO leads the development of a comprehensive risk assessment strategy, collaborates with cybersecurity experts to conduct thorough audits, and ensures that identified risks are promptly mitigated. It's very important for your team to review your policies and procedures to ensure they are adhering to all HIPAA requirements.

B. Secure Cloud Storage and Services

Utilizing cloud storage and services that comply with HIPAA regulations is vital. This includes ensuring that service providers sign business associate agreements (BAAs) and implement robust security measures. The CIO evaluates and selects cloud service providers based on their ability to meet HIPAA compliance standards, collaborates with legal teams to establish BAAs, and monitors the security posture of cloud services regularly.

C. Employee Training and Awareness Programs

Conducting regular training programs for hospital staff on HIPAA regulations is imperative. Employees need to be aware of their roles and responsibilities in maintaining compliance and the importance of data privacy and security. Develop and oversee a comprehensive training program, integrating technology-specific modules to educate staff on the secure use of digital tools and systems, and track the effectiveness of training initiatives.

D. Incident Response and Breach Notification Plans

Establishing detailed incident response and breach notification plans is essential for a swift and effective response to security incidents. This involves protocols for investigating breaches, notifying affected parties, and implementing corrective actions. Develop and regularly test incident response plans, ensuring that IT systems support rapid identification and containment of security incidents. More details on these in chapter 8.

E. Continuous Monitoring and Updates

Your organization should implement continuous monitoring systems to detect and respond to security threats in real time. Regularly updating and patching software addresses vulnerabilities and ensures that systems are up to date with the latest security measures.

F. Documentation and Recordkeeping

Maintaining detailed documentation of security policies, procedures, and risk assessments is crucial for demonstrating compliance. This includes keeping records of access logs, security incidents, and corrective actions taken.

* * *

In conclusion, navigating the complex terrain of compliance and regulatory frameworks is not just a duty; it is a strategic imperative. HIPAA guides our decisions and shapes the trajectory of our technological advancements. By integrating compliance seamlessly into our IT strategy, investing in robust security infrastructure, and fostering a culture of continual improvement, we not only ensure the sanctity of patient data but also fortify the foundation upon which our hospital's digital future stands.

CHAPTER 7:
NIST AND CIS FRAMEWORKS

The National Institute of Standards and Technology (NIST) and the Center for Internet Security (CIS) are prominent organizations offering cybersecurity frameworks and guidelines, yet they diverge in focus and methodology. NIST, a nonregulatory federal agency under the US Department of Commerce, develops standards, guidelines, and best practices to bolster information systems' security across various sectors. The NIST Cybersecurity Framework (CSF) emphasizes a flexible, risk-based approach structured around five core functions: identify, protect, detect, respond, and recover. This adaptable framework allows organizations to manage cybersecurity risks systematically, catering to diverse organizational structures and risk profiles.

Conversely, the Center for Internet Security (CIS), a nonprofit entity, concentrates on enhancing global cybersecurity readiness and response. CIS offers the CIS Controls, a set of prioritized security measures grouped into three categories: basic, foundational, and organizational. These controls provide specific, actionable guidelines for safeguarding against common cyber threats. While both NIST and CIS frameworks are voluntary and not regulatory requirements, they are widely recognized as industry best practices. NIST's collaborative development process involves industry stakeholders and cybersecurity experts, while CIS operates as a community-driven organization, fostering collaboration among cybersecurity professionals and partners. Organizations can benefit from leveraging both NIST and

CIS frameworks to tailor comprehensive cybersecurity strategies to their unique needs and objectives.

NIST Framework

The National Institute of Standards and Technology (NIST) Cybersecurity Framework provides a comprehensive approach to managing cybersecurity risk, offering a structured set of guidelines, best practices, and standards that organizations can use to assess and improve their cybersecurity posture. At its core, the NIST framework is built upon the five key functions mentioned earlier: identify, protect, detect, respond, and recover. These functions serve as the cornerstone of a robust cybersecurity strategy, guiding organizations through the process of assessing risk, implementing protective measures, detecting and responding to threats, and recovering from cybersecurity incidents.

The first step in incorporating the NIST framework into a cybersecurity program is to conduct a thorough assessment of an organization's cybersecurity posture. This involves identifying and cataloging assets, assessing vulnerabilities, and evaluating existing cybersecurity controls. By gaining a clear understanding of risks and vulnerabilities, you can prioritize your efforts and allocate resources effectively.

Once you have identified your cybersecurity risks, the next step is to implement protective measures to mitigate those risks. This may involve implementing access controls, encryption, and other security measures to safeguard sensitive patient data. It also includes establishing policies and procedures to govern the secure use of technology within your organization, such as employee training and awareness programs.

The *detect* function of the NIST framework focuses on the timely detection of cybersecurity events. To achieve this, you leverage a combination of automated tools, such as intrusion detection systems and security information and event management (SIEM) solutions, as well as manual monitoring and analysis by the cybersecurity team.

By continuously monitoring systems and networks for signs of unauthorized activity, you can detect and respond to threats in a timely manner.

For the *respond* function, in case of a cybersecurity incident, the NIST framework provides guidelines on how to contain the incident, mitigate its impact, and restore normal operations. This involves information to be included in the incident response plan, as well as the disaster recovery procedures.

Finally, the recover function of the NIST framework focuses on restoring services and mitigating the impact of a cybersecurity incident. This may involve restoring from backups, rebuilding compromised systems, and implementing corrective actions to prevent similar incidents from occurring in the future.

Incorporating the NIST framework into our cybersecurity program is not a one-time effort but an ongoing process. It requires continual assessment, adaptation, and improvement to ensure that our organization remains resilient in the face of evolving cybersecurity threats. By leveraging the NIST framework as a guiding framework, you can strengthen your cybersecurity posture, safeguard patient data, and uphold the trust and confidence of your patients and stakeholders.

CIS Framework

CIS Controls serve as a comprehensive framework guiding our cybersecurity strategy. By prioritizing these controls, we can systematically assess our current security posture and identify areas for improvement. This allows us to allocate resources efficiently, focusing on measures that offer the greatest impact in mitigating common cyber threats.

Implementing CIS Controls across our hospital's systems and devices is instrumental in strengthening our security infrastructure. From securing network devices to implementing robust access controls, each measure contributes to enhancing our overall cybersecurity resilience. Moreover, aligning our security practices with CIS recommendations ensures compliance with industry regulations, such as HIPAA, demonstrating our commitment to safeguarding patient data and meeting regulatory requirements.

Conducting annual security posture assessments (SPAs) and security risk assessments (SRAs) based on CIS guidelines provides us with invaluable insights into potential vulnerabilities and threats. These assessments enable us to proactively manage cybersecurity risks, develop risk mitigation strategies, and prepare robust incident response plans.

The goal is to mature our program every year, increasing the level of CIS Controls as necessary. Ultimately, continual monitoring, assessment, and improvement based on CIS benchmarks empower us to stay ahead of evolving cyber threats and maintain the trust and confidence of our patients and stakeholders.

CHAPTER 8:

INCIDENT RESPONSE PLAN AND DISASTER RECOVERY PROCEDURES

The significance of incident response plans and disaster recovery procedures in the cybersecurity foundation cannot be emphasized enough. These plans serve as proactive and reactive strategies, designed to prevent, detect, and mitigate the impact of security incidents, ranging from data breaches to ransomware attacks. Effective incident response procedures are not just a best practice; they are also a fundamental requirement for the modern health-care landscape, helping hospitals protect both their patients and their reputations.

To this end, we decided to take a slightly different approach. Instead of having the standard technical incident response playbook most organizations have, I asked my team to help create two different ones. The first is the standard tactical response team incident response plan, which delves into the technical nuances of incident response. The second is a command center incident response plan that provides a high-level overview for our leadership team, allowing them to remain abreast of the technical work and guide our response to cybersecurity incidents. Together, these plans equip our organization to efficiently navigate the complex world of cybersecurity threats.

Command Center Incident Response Plan

Our command center incident response plan serves as a guiding light for the hospital's leadership team during cybersecurity incidents. In the health-care space, we encounter cyber threats on an almost weekly basis, and often the nontechnical team feels out of the loop as we decipher the severity of attacks. A playbook created specifically for them helps alleviate their confusion and helps them make decisions more effectively.

While our technical teams focus on the intricate details of cybersecurity incident response, this plan allows our executives to provide valuable resources and guidance to our dedicated cybersecurity incident response team (CIRT). It ensures that our leadership remains informed and ready to make strategic decisions. The playbook includes checklists for our key executives, including all members of senior leadership. It works in conjunction with the tactical response team incident response plan, guiding the remediation process, recovery of affected systems, and reporting procedures required by law.

Both plans adhere to the best practices defined in the National Institute of Standards and Technology (NIST) incident response life cycle, consisting of five stages: preparation, detection and analysis, containment, eradication and recovery, and postincident activity. Each stage is comprehensively covered in both plans, offering guidance from both a technical and a leadership perspective.

The Power of Dual Playbooks
Speed and Efficiency

Technical teams can act swiftly using the tactical response team incident response plan to contain and mitigate threats. Simultaneously, our executives can focus on their roles with the guidance of the command center incident response plan, ensuring the hospital's broader stability during an incident.

Specialized Expertise
Each playbook caters to the specific expertise and responsibilities of its intended audience. This ensures clarity in roles, minimizing the risk of confusion or miscommunication during a crisis.

Legal Compliance and Reputation Management
The command center incident response plan helps executives navigate legal and regulatory complexities while managing public relations, and safeguarding our hospital's reputation.

Our dual playbooks, the command center incident response plan for leadership and the tactical response team incident response plan for technical teams, exemplify our commitment to efficient and effective cybersecurity incident response. By adopting these plans, we empower our teams to act swiftly and decisively, ensuring minimal disruption to patient care and organizational stability. In an era of ever-evolving cyber threats, these playbooks are not just advisable; they are also essential for safeguarding the future of health care at our hospital.

Disaster Recovery Procedures
In parallel, disaster recovery procedures serve as a safety net to mitigate the impact of catastrophic events, such as natural disasters, infrastructure failures, or large-scale cyberattacks. These plans encompass strategies for restoring critical systems and data infrastructure to full functionality, thereby minimizing downtime and ensuring continuity of patient care.

For a large hospital system, where downtime can have life-threatening consequences, the ability to recover swiftly from disruptions is paramount. Disaster recovery plans outline predefined procedures for data backup, restoration, and failover to redundant systems, ensuring that essential services remain accessible even in the face of adversity.

Furthermore, comprehensive incident response and disaster recovery plans play a pivotal role in regulatory compliance, particularly in the health-care sector, which is governed by stringent data protection laws, such as the Health Insurance Portability and Accountability Act (HIPAA). By demonstrating a proactive approach to cybersecurity preparedness, hospitals can mitigate regulatory penalties, safeguard their reputations, and maintain the trust of patients and stakeholders.

CHAPTER 9:

MEDICAL DEVICES AND CYBER THREATS

A s you all know, medical devices play an important role in health care. They help assess, evaluate, diagnose, manage, and treat patients daily. However, as these devices become more sophisticated and more connected to the web, they will also become prime targets for cybercriminals. Cyberattacks on medical devices can be devastating and dangerous. They can jeopardize patient care, disrupt clinical operations, and expose sensitive information. That's why it is important to build and maintain a resilient cybersecurity infrastructure to protect these devices from threats.

So what threats are we talking about here? There are several that deserve serious consideration:

1. *Unauthorized Access*: Hackers attempt to gain physical or remote access to hospital medical devices to interfere with their operations or steal their data.

2. *Malware Infection*: Like computers, medical devices can be infected with viruses, worms, or ransomware. These can compromise their functionality or even encrypt data for ransom.

3. *Denial of Service (DoS) Attacks*: Cybercriminals will attempt to overwhelm medical devices, hack them online, or disrupt their normal operation.

4. *Data Breaches*: Attackers will try to target sensitive patient information stored or transmitted through medical devices, thereby violating privacy and creating legal problems.

The question to ask yourself while reading is how to keep these devices safe. Well, you need to implement a comprehensive cybersecurity strategy, and here are some key considerations:

1. Risk Assessment and Management

Hospitals should frequently assess their medical devices for risks and vulnerabilities, and they should keep detailed records of all devices and software used, the exposure between them, and where data flows in and out. Being aware of your environment internally and externally is important.

2. Access Control and Authentication

Using strong authentication methods, such as multifactor authentication, can help restrict unauthorized access to medical devices. And hospitals have to figure out who can get what–give people only the absolute minimum rights they need based on their roles. "Least privileged" is the way to go.

3. Network Segmentation and Monitoring

Separating the medical device network from other hospital networks is a smart move. This reduces the number of entry points for hackers and limits how far they can go if a system is breached. Hospitals should also implement intrusion detection and prevention systems to monitor web traffic and identify potential cyber threats.

4. Secure Updates and Patching

Device manufacturers also play a big role. Security should be launched in the development process from the beginning, and patches should be launched quickly when vulnerabilities are discovered. On the clinical side, they need a robust way to test and deploy those screens quickly without disrupting the patient-care workflow. Falling behind the trail is just asking for trouble.

5. Data Encryption and Backups

Any sensitive patient data stored or transmitted on medical devices must be encrypted to protect privacy. And you can't forget about backups—hospitals should securely back up critical data regularly and make sure those backups are sound. If things are going sideways, you don't want to be caught without a reliable backup.

6. Incident Response and Recovery

Even with the most expensive preventive measures, computer incidents can still happen. This is why having an incident response system geared to detect, prevent, and recover from attacks on medical devices is nonnegotiable. Health-care systems should also be equipped with redundant systems or alternative procedures to maintain continuity of care in such cases.

7. Awareness and Training

This isn't just about technology, though. Health-care staff at all levels need regular cybersecurity awareness training to help them understand policies, identify risks, and report suspicious activity. Building that security-minded culture and vigilance throughout the organization is vital for thwarting threats to medical devices.

When it comes down to it, protecting medical devices from cyberattacks and threats requires an all-hands-on-deck approach (as we call it in the military). We need a collaborative effort between health-care providers, device manufacturers, regulatory bodies, and cybersecurity experts. Hospitals must regularly conduct risk assessments, monitor, and use proactive security measures to safeguard these devices and ensure patient safety in the face of an ever-evolving cyber world.

That is why having the biomedical department work hand in hand with the IT department under the leadership of a CIO makes more sense these days. Medical devices are getting smarter and more connected to hospital networks and systems—it's becoming harder to separate medical technology from the IT side of things.

At my hospital, I convinced my executive team to have the biomedical team be a part of the IT department to make sure these connected devices are properly integrated, sharing data securely, and protected from cyber threats. We're talking about patient safety and privacy here, so getting the cybersecurity measures correct is crucial.

My IT department and my cybersecurity team have outstanding skills when it comes to cybersecurity best practices, risk assessments, and handling incidents. But the biomedical team knows the ins and outs of the medical devices themselves—how they work, what they're used for clinically, the whole nine yards. Combining that expertise was key.

And let's not forget the network design itself. Medical devices need robust and secure communication infrastructure to communicate and share data. That's the domain of the IT department—to manage and secure those critical network infrastructures for devices to function properly. In addition, maintaining all the hospital's assets—whether it's computers, servers, or medical equipment—is a big deal. Integrating biomedical IT teams allows for streamlined asset management, better planning for replacement and upgrades, and more efficient resource utilization.

At the end of the day, electronic medical devices require multiple approaches. IT and biomedical professionals must collaborate, share knowledge, and train—that's how you develop a comprehensive plan to protect these critical devices and keep patients safe in our increasingly tech-driven health-care world.

CHAPTER 10:

ARTIFICIAL INTELLIGENCE (AI) IN HEALTH CARE

The swift progress in artificial intelligence (AI) technology is causing a revolution in the health-care sector. AI has the power to completely transform a number of facets of health care, including patient-care delivery and clinical decision-making. Health-care providers can discover new opportunities in early disease detection, individualized treatment plans, operational efficiency, and improved patient outcomes by utilizing AI-powered tools and algorithms. As artificial intelligence (AI) develops, its incorporation into the health-care system has the potential to enable more accurate, data-driven, and efficient health-care services, ultimately raising the standard of patient care. The following are a number of ways health-care systems stand to gain greatly from the application of AI:

1. Disease Diagnosis and Treatment Planning

AI algorithms are able to analyze vast amounts of medical data, such as test results, medical images, and symptoms, in order to help with personalized treatment planning and accurate disease diagnosis. Artificial intelligence (AI) can help physicians make better decisions by spotting patterns and correlations.

2. Drug Discovery and Development

By evaluating enormous volumes of biological data, modeling molecular interactions, and more quickly identifying possible drug candidates than with conventional techniques, AI can speed up the process of drug discovery and development.

3. Personalized Medicine

AI can assist in creating treatment regimens that are specifically catered to each patient, taking into account the patient's genetic composition, past medical conditions, and other variables. This may result in targeted, more potent treatments with fewer adverse effects.

4. Medical Imaging Analysis

By precisely identifying abnormalities, tumors, or other conditions that may be challenging for human experts to spot, AI can improve the analysis of medical imaging data, such as X-rays, CT scans, and MRI scans.

5. Predictive Analytics

AI is able to forecast possible health risks, the course of a disease, and the chance of readmissions or unfavorable events by analyzing patient data, including electronic health records. This can aid in the prevention of disease and more efficient use of resources by health-care providers.

6. Virtual Assistants and Chatbots

These AI-powered tools can help patients with appointment scheduling, prescription refilling, chronic condition management, and personalized information. They can also respond to common medical questions.

7. Robotic Surgery

Artificial intelligence (AI) can improve robotic surgical systems' accuracy and precision, allowing for more intricate and minimally invasive procedures that have better results and quicker patient recovery times.

8. Clinical Decision Support

Artificial intelligence (AI) systems can help medical professionals by reducing human error and treatment inconsistencies, providing real-time decision support, and making recommendations based on the most recent medical knowledge.

Even though AI has a lot of potential, ethical issues must be addressed, data security and privacy must be guaranteed, and human oversight and control must be preserved in crucial decision-making processes within health-care systems.

AI and Cybersecurity in Health Care

Health care is embracing AI more and more, but at the same time, the industry is having to deal with an ever-growing threat from cyberattacks. With sophisticated tactics, malicious actors are focusing on health-care organizations in an attempt to take advantage of weaknesses and obtain unauthorized access to vital systems and private patient data. AI-powered cybersecurity solutions are becoming a vital line of defense in this environment. AI-based systems can mitigate the effects of ransomware attacks and data breaches by utilizing machine learning algorithms and predictive analytics to detect and respond to cyber threats instantly. AI can also improve the effectiveness of security operations by automating vulnerability management, incident response, and threat detection. This helps health-care organizations protect their digital infrastructure and stay one step ahead of cybercriminals.

The following are some ways AI can improve health-care cyber-security

1. Threat Detection and Prevention

AI algorithms are more effective than conventional techniques at identifying potential cyber threats by analyzing massive volumes of data from a variety of sources, including network traffic, user behavior, and system logs. AI makes it possible to identify irregularities, questionable patterns, and signs of compromise early on, preventing cyberattacks.

2. Vulnerability Management

AI can help prioritize and find software flaws, incorrect set-ups, and vulnerabilities in health-care systems. AI can assist enterprises in proactively mitigating risks and patching vulnerabilities more quickly by continuously monitoring and analyzing system data.

3. User and Entity Behavior Analytics (UEBA)

By creating baselines for typical user and system behavior, AI-powered UEBA solutions make it possible to identify unusual activity that could be a sign of insider threats, compromised accounts, or illegal access attempts.

4. Predictive Analytics

AI can forecast prospective future attacks and their vectors by analyzing historical cyber threat data, security incidents, and other pertinent data. Health-care companies can more wisely use their resources and fortify their security posture with the aid of this predictive capability.

5. Automated Response and Remediation

In the event of a cyberattack, AI can help with automated response and remediation procedures. AI systems are able to suggest or launch suitable countermeasures, like patching and updating, isolating compromised systems, or obstructing malicious traffic, based on their analysis of the attack's nature and extent.

6. Constant Monitoring and Adaptation

AI can keep an eye out for updates, changes, and new vulnerabilities in health-care systems and adjust policies and security measures accordingly. By using a dynamic approach, organizations can remain ahead of the ever-evolving cyber threats.

7. Security Orchestration and Automation

Artificial intelligence has the ability to automate and orchestrate a range of security processes, including threat hunting, incident response, and security operations. This lessens the workload for security teams and allows for quicker and more efficient response times.

When organizations are using AI for cybersecurity in health care, it is crucial to take into account potential issues like data privacy, algorithmic bias, and the requirement for human oversight and governance. Working together, cybersecurity specialists, AI experts, and health-care stakeholders can guarantee the responsible and successful application of AI in this vital field.

CHAPTER 11:

MASTERING THE CYBERSECURITY LIFE CYCLE

Health-care organizations must adopt a comprehensive and organized strategy in the constantly changing field of cybersecurity. With the help of the cybersecurity life cycle, executives can efficiently detect, mitigate, and respond to cyber threats in a proactive manner. Health-care executives may strengthen their defenses, protect vital resources, and keep the confidence of stakeholders and patients by comprehending and putting this life cycle's fundamental ideas into practice.

Proactive Risk Management
By placing a strong emphasis on proactive threat identification and mitigation, the life cycle approach helps organizations reduce their vulnerability to cyberattacks and stay ahead of possible risks.

Comprehensive Asset Protection
Health-care organizations can prevent unauthorized access to or compromise of proprietary information, medical devices, and sensitive patient data by carefully mapping and safeguarding critical assets.

Enhanced Incident Response

Health-care executives can guarantee a coordinated and effective response to cyber incidents, minimizing downtime and potential patient harm, by putting in place well-defined incident response protocols.

Regulatory Compliance

By conforming to industry norms and legal mandates like HIPAA and NIST guidelines, the cybersecurity life cycle assists health-care organizations in staying compliant and avoiding expensive fines.

Constant Learning, Adaptation, and Improvement

The iterative nature of the life cycle promotes constant learning, adaptation, and improvement, making sure that your company's cybersecurity posture stays strong and in line with best practices and emerging threats.

Developing a Culture of Cybersecurity

The cybersecurity life cycle implementation process involves more than just technical work; it also calls for an organizational culture change. Health-care executives need to be leaders in cybersecurity awareness and create a culture where all staff members are aware of their responsibilities for safeguarding sensitive information and systems. A strong cybersecurity culture requires consistent training, open communication, and demonstrable leadership commitment.

Health-care executives can confidently navigate the complex landscape of cyber threats by adopting the cybersecurity life cycle, thereby safeguarding their organizations, preserving patient trust, and guaranteeing the uninterrupted provision of essential health-care services. While building cyber resilience is an ongoing process, you can strengthen your defenses and stay ahead of the curve when it comes to emerging cyber threats by following this all-inclusive framework.

SECTION 3: COLLABORATIVE APPROACHES TO CYBERSECURITY

CHAPTER 12:

BUILDING A TEAM

In today's competitive market, where organizations are vying for the same pool of talented professionals, hiring the right individuals with the appropriate skill sets is crucial. However, I firmly believe that hiring for attitude is even more important. In this section, we will explore strategies for building a strong cybersecurity team in this challenging market by emphasizing the importance of attitude, continual learning, and effective leadership.

Navigating the Competitive Market

In an environment where everyone is searching for the same skilled individuals, it becomes essential to explore alternative avenues for talent acquisition. Collaborating with HR departments, partnering with recruiting companies, tapping into military talent, engaging retirees, and connecting with educational organizations can help broaden the pool of potential candidates. By diversifying our recruitment efforts, we increase our chances of finding individuals with the right attitude and aptitude for cybersecurity.

Emphasizing the Right Attitude

While technical skills are undoubtedly important, hiring for attitude is paramount. The right attitude encompasses a mindset that values training and a willingness to learn, as cybersecurity is a rapidly evolving field. By prioritizing candidates who demonstrate a hunger for continual growth, we ensure that our team remains adaptable and capable of handling emerging threats.

Hiring as a Relationship

Hiring is not just about skills and qualifications; it is also about finding a mutual fit. Just as in a relationship, it is crucial to assess whether the candidate's attitude complements that of the existing team. Building a cohesive unit involves assembling individuals who bring diverse perspectives, strengths, and values. This collaborative spirit fosters innovation and resilience in the face of cyber challenges.

Retaining and Nurturing Talent

When we come across exceptional talent, it is important to hold on to it, even if there is not an immediate job opening. Good talent with the right attitude is difficult to come by. By bringing in talented individuals and providing them with training and growth opportunities, we invest in the long-term success of both the team and the organization. We should also consider giving newbies a chance, along with existing team members who are interested in growing horizontally, as experience is not always a prerequisite for success. A fresh perspective can invigorate the team and bring new insights to the table.

Developing Effective Leadership

Building the right team also entails fostering effective leadership. As leaders, we must adopt an open-door policy and actively connect with our team members. Creating a culture of continual learning and improvement involves teaching leaders to be better leaders themselves. Sharing knowledge and empowering team members through a "manage-up" approach, where everyone is encouraged to teach and learn from others, cultivates a sense of ownership and drives professional growth within the team.

Fairness and Inclusion

A strong team is built on fairness and inclusion. Every team member requires a different style of leadership, and it is important to provide equal opportunities for growth and development. Encouraging open communication, embracing feedback, and treating every team member with respect and fairness fosters a positive work environment and strengthens the bond within the team.

By valuing the right mindset, prioritizing continual learning, and fostering effective leadership, we create an environment where talented professionals can thrive. Embracing alternative recruitment channels, such as HR departments, recruiting companies, military bases, retiree communities, and schools, expands our talent pool and increases the chances of finding individuals who possess the necessary skills and the attitude required to excel in the ever-evolving field of cybersecurity.

CHAPTER 13:

CONSULTANT PARTNERSHIPS

It is particularly important to find the right consulting partner, especially in the realm of cybersecurity. Many consultants prioritize financial gains over personalized solutions, so it is crucial to seek out ethical, committed, and knowledgeable experts. In this section, I will highlight the key factors that make a good consultant, emphasizing the need for trust, a personal touch, and a focus on tailored solutions.

Seeking References and Personal Contacts

A reliable consultant should have no hesitation providing references from previous clients who can vouch for their professionalism and quality of work. However, do not rely solely on provided references; take the initiative to seek out your own contacts within the industry to gather additional insights into the consultant's reputation and performance.

Inquisitiveness and Calmness

The right consultant will ask thoughtful questions and remain calm, avoiding rushing into generic solutions. Their inquisitive nature demonstrates their commitment to understanding your organization's unique challenges and tailoring solutions accordingly.

Focus on Knowledge Transfer

A good consultant should not be interested in just providing a quick fix; they should be dedicated to transferring knowledge to your internal team. Empowering your staff with the necessary skills ensures that your organization can maintain the benefits of the consultant's expertise long after the engagement ends.

Establishing a Personal Connection

Building trust is vital for any successful consultant-client relationship. Seek a consultant who values a personal touch and loyalty to your organization's mission. A strong personal connection fosters a collaborative and supportive environment for achieving common goals.

Trial Period Evaluation

Consider implementing a trial period before committing to a long-term engagement. This allows both parties to assess compatibility, working styles, and expectations. The ninety-day relationship rule should apply to business as well—a trial period provides an opportunity to determine how well the consultant fits into your organization's culture and values. I knew after a couple of weeks of working with WIRED Security consultants that they were the right fit for our hospital system.

Creating Tailored Solutions

Beware of consultants who offer one-size-fits-all solutions. A reliable consultant will analyze your organization's specific challenges, objectives, and resources to create a customized cybersecurity program that aligns perfectly with your unique needs. When it comes to cybersecurity, ethical behavior is nonnegotiable. A trustworthy consultant must genuinely care about the security and well-being of your organization, putting your interests before their financial gains. Look for a partner who shares your ethical principles and values and is committed to protecting your organization from potential threats.

Choosing the right consultant for your cybersecurity needs is paramount to building a sustainable program that effectively protects your organization. Focus on ethics, trust, and personal connection, and seek out partners who are committed to providing tailored solutions and transferring knowledge. By doing so, you can ensure a successful and long-lasting consultant-client relationship that contributes to your organization's security and prosperity.

CHAPTER 14:

RELATIONSHIPS WITH LAW ENFORCEMENT AND OTHER GOVERNMENT AGENCIES

While there are specific state and federal regulations requiring businesses, especially health-care organizations, to contact law enforcement authorities when a criminal cybersecurity issue occurs, there aren't many concrete requirements for them to do so. However, if you as a CIO, a VP of IT, or a CISO suspect criminal activity or a breach, it is advisable to get in touch with a law enforcement agency as soon as possible.

The Department of Justice (DOJ) defines an incident as an occurrence that constitutes a violation or imminent threat of violation of security policies or security procedures or that actually or potentially jeopardizes the confidentiality, integrity, or availability of an information system. The DOJ also defines a breach as a situation where persons other than authorized users have access or potential access to information, whether physical or electronic. The term encompasses both external invasions and internal misuses within a company.

Long before you experience a cyber incident, I advise you to try building a rapport with the local, state, and federal law enforcement agencies in your area. If you need to enlist law enforcement's assistance, having a point of contact and an established relationship with them will make any subsequent interactions easier. Additionally, it will support the development of a trustworthy relationship that fosters information sharing in both directions, which is advantageous to law enforcement and your organization. Furthermore, you should have a preestablished secure communication channel with external law enforcement to share and discuss detection, response, and recovery steps, according to NIST Special Publication 800-184, *Guide for Cybersecurity Event Recovery*.

Prior to an incident, organizations, especially in health care, must establish contact with an FBI point of contact. No CIO or CISO should be speaking with the FBI for the first time when an incident has just occurred.

Being a retired law enforcement officer myself has been very beneficial to me in building ties with local, state, and federal law enforcement agencies in my area. The fact that I retired in the county where I work and know a lot of law enforcement and federal agents allows me to obtain information that is crucial to the safety of my health-care district.

You will need to put in extra effort to get in touch with and meet with every law enforcement agency in the area if you are a CIO or CISO and have never worked with law enforcement before.

It is imperative that you get in contact with your local law enforcement agency and locate the FBI field office, the CISA liaison for your area, and the liaison person(s) for cyber/internet crimes. Schedule a meeting with these individuals and get to know them; they possess important knowledge that they may share with you to safeguard your business.

Federal law enforcement agencies will typically have the most resources and capabilities available to them when it comes to investigating cybersecurity incidents. Under the Computer Fraud and Abuse Act, the Federal Bureau of Investigation (FBI) and the US Secret Service (USSS) are designated as having concurrent jurisdiction to investigate these incidents.

The FBI and USSS carry out regular outreach to private businesses and other organizations that might be the target of hacks and attacks. The main channels for this kind of outreach are the US Secret Service's

Electronic Crimes Task Forces and the FBI's InfraGard chapters and Cyber Task Forces in all field offices.

In addition to gathering and reporting on cyber incidents, phishing, malware, and other vulnerabilities, the Department of Homeland Security has cybersecurity-focused components that also offer specific incident response services. For the purpose of cybersecurity information sharing, incident response, and incident coordination, the National Cybersecurity and Communications Integration Center (NCCIC) is open around the clock. You can provide and receive information about an ongoing incident that could be helpful to the government and your organization by contacting the NCCIC. Additionally, you might be able to get technical support for containing an ongoing cyber incident.

My advice is to engage local, state, and federal law enforcement agencies prior to incidents; however, there are several justifications for collaborating and harvesting relationships with law enforcement agencies following a cybercrime incident.

Agencies have the authority to order third parties to provide information that is required to reconstruct the incident's sequence of events, thereby enhancing an organization's defenses.

In order to locate stolen data or identify the perpetrator, law enforcement may be able to enlist the aid of international law enforcement partners, as well as use legal authorities and tools that are not available to nongovernmental organizations. These resources and connections can significantly raise the likelihood of catching an attacker or intruder and protecting deleted data.

When regulators, shareholders, the public, and other external parties review a company's responses, early reporting to and cooperation with law enforcement will be given favorable consideration.

CHAPTER 15:

CYBER INSURANCE

The health-care industry has witnessed a staggering increase in cyberattacks in the last few years. In response to these escalating threats, cyber insurance has emerged as a vital risk management tool for health-care organizations. Unlike traditional insurance policies that primarily focus on physical assets, cyber insurance provides coverage for losses resulting from data breaches, ransomware attacks, and other cyber incidents. It serves as a financial safety net, helping organizations mitigate the financial fallout of a cyberattack, including costs associated with forensic investigations, regulatory fines, legal fees, and reputational damage.

Beyond financial protection, cyber insurance enables organizations to enhance their cybersecurity posture by incentivizing the implementation of robust security measures and incident response protocols. Insurance providers often offer risk assessment services, cybersecurity training programs, and access to cybersecurity experts, empowering health-care organizations to proactively identify and mitigate potential vulnerabilities.

By investing in cyber insurance, organizations signal their dedication to protecting patient data, thereby bolstering their reputations and credibility within the health-care community.

Furthermore, cyber insurance can be a catalyst for innovation and growth. In today's highly competitive health-care landscape, organizations that demonstrate robust cybersecurity practices are more likely to attract patients, partners, and investors. Cyber insurance coverage can serve as a competitive differentiator, providing organizations with a strategic advantage in an increasingly digitized marketplace.

When choosing cyber insurance, be sure not to have the decision be spearheaded by business executives only. The CIO and the CISO must both be present and heavily involved to ensure all their technical concerns are met when vetting a policy. As the CIO, I helped save my hospital system up to 150 percent off a policy because we were able to integrate feedback in real time.

As the health-care industry continues to embrace digital transformation, cyber insurance will undoubtedly play a pivotal role in ensuring the safety, security, and integrity of patient data and organizational assets.

CHAPTER 16:

VENDOR ASSESSMENTS

When conducting vendor assessments, hospitals must consider several key factors to ensure thorough evaluation and effective risk management. Here are some important things to keep in mind:

1. Identify Critical Vendors

Determine which vendors have access to sensitive patient data, provide essential services, or have a significant impact on hospital operations. Focus your assessment efforts on these critical vendors to prioritize risk management.

2. Define Assessment Criteria

Establish clear criteria for evaluating vendors, including cybersecurity practices, data protection measures, regulatory compliance, financial stability, reputation, and the quality of services provided. Tailor the assessment criteria to align with specific risks and requirements relevant to the health-care industry.

3. Review Security Practices

Assess the vendor's cybersecurity policies, procedures, and controls to ensure they align with industry best practices and regulatory standards, such as HIPAA. Evaluate aspects such as access controls, encryption, incident response plans, vulnerability management, and employee training programs.

4. Evaluate Data Protection Measures

Examine how the vendor handles and protects sensitive patient data. Verify that appropriate encryption, access controls, data retention policies, and data breach notification procedures are in place to safeguard patient confidentiality and comply with privacy regulations.

5. Assess Regulatory Compliance

Ensure that the vendor complies with relevant health-care regulations, such as HIPAA, General Data Protection Regulation (GDPR), and other industry-specific requirements. Request documentation and evidence of compliance, such as audit reports, certifications, and contractual assurances.

6. Assess Vendor Security Risks

Identify and assess potential security risks associated with the vendor, such as cybersecurity vulnerabilities, past security incidents, reliance on subcontractors, and geographic location. Conduct thorough risk assessments to understand the impact and likelihood of these risks and develop mitigation strategies accordingly.

7. Foreground Contractual Considerations

Draft contracts and service-level agreements (SLAs) that include robust cybersecurity clauses, data protection provisions, indemnification clauses, breach notification requirements, and auditing rights. Clearly define each party's responsibilities, liabilities, and obligations regarding cybersecurity and data protection.

8. Ensure Continual Monitoring and Oversight

Implement mechanisms for ongoing monitoring and oversight of vendors to ensure compliance with security requirements and contractual obligations. Regularly review vendor performance, conduct periodic security assessments, and maintain open communication channels to address any emerging risks or issues promptly.

9. Implement a Vendor Management Program

Establish a comprehensive vendor management program that out-lines procedures for vendor selection, assessment, onboarding, monitoring, and termination. Assign roles and responsibilities within the organization for overseeing vendor relationships and cybersecurity governance.

10. Document and Maintain Records

Keep detailed documentation of the vendor assessment process, including assessment reports, contracts, communications, and audit trails. Maintain accurate records of vendor relationships, security assessments, compliance status, and any remediation efforts undertaken.

By considering these factors and implementing a structured approach to vendor assessment, hospitals can effectively manage third-party risks, protect patient data, ensure regulatory compliance, and strengthen their overall cybersecurity posture.

CONCLUSION

As we conclude this cybersecurity playbook, it's crucial to understand that safeguarding any organization, especially in health care, against cyber threats is an ongoing battle that demands vigilance, adaptability, and a steadfast commitment from leadership. The stakes have never been higher, with patient safety, data integrity, and organizational reputation hanging in the balance.

In today's interconnected world, a single vulnerability can have devastating consequences, jeopardizing not only the operations of your health-care facility but also the trust of the community you serve. Cybercriminals are relentless in their exploitation of weaknesses, driven by motives ranging from financial gain to malicious disruption.

But you can strengthen your defenses, foster a cybersecurity-aware culture, and set up reliable incident response procedures by putting the tactics in this playbook into practice.

To all my executive readers or anyone aspiring to be a leader, remember that making investments in cybersecurity is essential to safeguarding both the resiliency of your company and the health of your patients. It's not just a question of compliance.

Recall that cybersecurity is a journey rather than a destination. Your defenses must advance along with technology. Adopt a proactive stance, regularly reevaluate your weaknesses, keep up with new threats, and work with regulatory agencies and industries.

To all my CIOs and CISOs, keep in mind that although the road ahead may be difficult, with the correct attitude, tools, and unshakable commitment, you can successfully traverse the constantly shifting cybersecurity landscape and protect the priceless assets entrusted to your care. Accept this duty with fortitude and tenacity, as doing so will safeguard your company and improve the general well-being of the people and communities you serve.

ACKNOWLEDGMENTS

The process of writing this book has been amazing, and I will always be appreciative of all the people who helped me along the way. First and foremost, I would like to express my gratitude to my wife and three lovely children for their understanding, patience, and unwavering faith in me throughout the many hours and sacrifices needed to see this project through to completion. My constant source of inspiration has been your love and support.

I must thank Kj Grinde of WIRED Security Inc. from the bottom of my heart. He is the greatest cybersecurity partner, and he kindly gave his time, knowledge, and practical experience to me. His advice has been crucial in helping me become the IT/cyber professional I am today and in making sure that the information in this book is still applicable, current, and reflective of the difficulties encountered in the industry.

I also owe a great deal of gratitude to Komal Kapoor, who served as my mentor and writing coach. Komal's advice was priceless; it kept me motivated and focused while guiding me through the challenging process of writing a book. Komal's abilities and commitment were crucial in making this book a reality. Because of her intense attention to detail, her love of writing gripping stories, and her steadfast dedication to accuracy, each chapter has a rich and meaningful resonance. Beyond just being a talented writer, Komal was also very helpful because she pushed me to think critically and express myself clearly. Her collaboration and the numerous hours she dedicated to this project are greatly appreciated.

Last, I hope that every reader who picks up this book will be empowered by the knowledge it contains to navigate the constantly changing cybersecurity landscape with resilience, confidence, and the knowledge that you are a part of a committed community working to safeguard our digital world. It is an honor to be a part of this continuing mission, and this book is a testament to the collaborative spirit that characterizes our field.

9 798822 954434